The Death of a Lie

By

Phillitia Charlton

Published by

Charlton · Charlton Publishing
Dayton, OH
CharltonCharlton.com

charlton•charlton
PUBLISHING, INC.

Charlton · Charlton Publishing
Dayton, OH
CharltonCharlton.com

Scriptures were taken from the New International Version of the Holy Bible.

Library of Congress Control Number: 2017918076

ISBN-13: 978-0-9992269-0-2

Cover illustrated by Ronald Duckett
Cover designed by JD&J Design LLC
Edited by Lynel Johnson Washington and Natasha Hayes

Printed in the United States of America

Dedication

This book is dedicated to Eric, Dy'Oni & Eryk.

You are the people who encourage me to continue to dream and believe in the impossible.

To Pastor Joyce & Bishop Robinson and Mr. Alvin & Shirley Freeman; thank you for telling me to have the courage and the faith to tell my story so I can truly be free.

Table of Contents

Phillitia Charlton

Introduction

My perception of me was a false reality.
That perception had to die.
Welcome to the death of my lie.

Far too often we lie. No matter how cute, educated, professional or sanctified we claim to be, we lie. A lie is a lie even if you are only telling it to yourself. The older we get the further away we want to be from our past experiences. We often withhold the truth, our truth, at the expense of healing, uplifting and empowering ourselves and others.

My pastor, Joyce Robinson, always says, "Girl, go back and get me a piece of yesterday." She would wittingly say, "Go ahead, I'll wait." She knew what some never acknowledge or accept, she knew, that you just can't go back to fix it.

As I looked at each day as a blessing, I understood the gift of the present. As I reflect on my past struggles with validation, self-confidence, relationships and abandonment, I am beginning to understand some of my "whys". Until recently I never thought about how being abandoned and adopted at the age of five effected my perception of me and the world. When I was making it do what it do in college, I didn't attribute my "I'm doing me" attitude to not having a father around or the fact that

11

I lived in eight homes as my mother struggled with drug addiction, trauma, mental illness and homelessness. I created a customized super hero suit of lies to protect me from the consequences of my actions. College gave me the opportunity to try out all of my lies. I told myself that I didn't care what anyone thought. I told myself that I was in control. I told myself that being academically smart meant that I didn't have to have a moral compass. My sword of deception, my helmet of anger and my breast plate of denial helped me unsuccessfully go from relationship to relationship. And trust me; I am using the word relationship loosely. *The Death of a Lie* is my open college diary. Walking in my truth and facing myself in my writing has led me to a place of peace. Making mistakes does not make anyone a mistake, even at your ugliest. I am opening my diary in hopes that you will reminisce with me, grow with me and find yourself in our common experiences. Through every poem I didn't know I was getting stronger and stronger. As you read this work, if you find yourself in it, embrace your past with me. Rest assured the past is not coming back. Take a deep breath and let it go.

—Phillitia

Prelude

Phillitia Charlton

Split – The First One

My being is split into three
It's exposed like an open wound
With no chance of healing
My secret is out
I can play no more games
Three women reside in me
Who all have the same name
The first one
She's a sexy
Caramel chocolate dream
Brick House starts playing
Every time she hits the scene
Hour glass figure; even after two kids
She eludes confidence
It seeps from her pours
Acting as an aphrodisiac
Distinguishing her as a rose amongst thorns
Well-educated
Intelligent conversation
Conversation that stimulates the mind
An enchanting smile
One that captures a moment in time
That girl right there is a ten
She is the ultimate example
Of what men refer to as a dime
Her natural beauty captures the room
That woman who people can't stop talking about
It's me!

Phillitia Charlton

Split – The Second One

The second one is mad as hell
Angry at the world
Pissed about her childhood
Doesn't even remember being a girl
Hate dwells in her heart because
Life is just too damn hard
Always defensive
Stays on guard
She's gotta protect herself
From the cruel people of this world
She has to fight to stay alive
Every day is a battle and damn it
She will survive
She uses words
They cut like swords
Don't get in her way because
She will knock you down
Tell a joke that she thinks is not funny and
You will get clowned
She sees your agenda
As soon as you get in her face
Flashes from being beat as a child
So fresh in her head
They could never be erased
Protective walls shield her heart
Personal memories
Worse than horror films justify her behavior
They make it feel right

The Death of a Lie

When you speak to her
Choose your words carefully
Because she will fight
She learned as a child
To fight her bipolar parent
How to use words as weapons
Throws them like daggers
That penetrate through,
So please tell me
Why don't you think
She will lay into you
The ones she loved
Have betrayed her the most
So how could she trust someone new
To do anything other than mess her over
Cause that's what she's used to
So put your loving word(s), embracing arms,
Gentle eyes and soft-spoken lies away
They fuel her anger
They put the unleashed beast
Inside her on the prowl
This beast is more deadly than Jason
Scarier than Freddie
More complex than Alien
So go ahead, play with her
Make her angry if you want to
Don't ask the first one
To help with the second one
The anger puts all her rationale away
The third one is too damn scared
She won't dare get in the way

Phillitia Charlton

So if you bring out the second one
I just suggest you run
Because hate is being fired from
A semi-automatic weapon
From behind the wall
That guards what is left of her heart
She will shoot you and not think twice
She will never hurt again
If it takes for you to die
Then start making funeral plans

Split – The Last One

The third one is as insecure as a lost little girl
Haunted by stretch marks
She believes they took her sexiness away
Turns the lights down in intimacy
She's too afraid
Hoping that love is enough to make him stay
Looks in the mirror
She doesn't understand
Wants to regain the love of herself
Without a man
Views her body as scary
Where everything is disheveled or misplaced
Constantly weary of looking at the lazy eye
That causes her to feel disgraced
Compares herself to everyone and
Always comes up short
Failing miserably at this life mission
Seeking ways to abort
Embarrassed by her crack-head mother
Who still roams the streets
Head down
Unable to take compliments
From the people she meets
A procrastinator
She doesn't believe dreams can come true
Most of the time good people come in last
That's just a reality she has to get used to
Nothing she does is good enough

No matter what people say
Victimization and fear are the cinderblocks
She puts in her own way
What if she can't make it
All the twists and turns of life
What if she can't take it
What if people only remember her
For what she used to be
Is that a reflection of all she will ever be
She wished she had the appeal of the first one
The first one, Beauty is her name
The second one is just as bad
Her fierceness cannot be tamed
But the third one is a mere shell of a woman
With no substance in between
Trapped in her own nightmare of low-esteem

Part One:

Writing and Rapping in the Attic

Phillitia Charlton

1989: A Poem for My Mother

Crack is a substance used by idiots
It makes your hair fall out
And now you look hideous
Standing on the corner,
Went out into the street,
A man rode by and said, "Look at that geek!"
You weighed 163 now you're down to 90
You thought you were in front,
But now you're behind me
Taking that razor blade
Grinding it up,
Barking and begging as if you were a mutt
You're already classified in a little section
Come on let us help
And give you some direction
Together we can lick it, just like that
Stick with us and we'll get you off that crack
Take it from us our advice is for real
Now will you or won't you take that deal?

Phillitia Charlton

Love Gone By – Rap 1989

I did my best to treat you right
I tried to love you with all of my might
You cold dissed me
You plain dismissed me
And when you did it I started to cry
The tear drops fell right from my eyes
I said you dead wrong
You said what did I do
I said you hurt me, baby, that ain't even cool

I still love you and I don't why
I guess the feelings that I had inside
Never went bye-bye
I don't play when it comes to love
Because you are like a gift sent from up above
I want you back but I know I can't have you
Listen to my rhyme and please let it grab you
Let it hold you tight
The way you used to hold me
I miss you, baby, can't you see
My love is stronger than a thousand bolts of thunder

I'm coming to the conclusion
The end of my rhyme
I'm gonna love you, baby
Until the end of time
All I have to say is L-O-V-E
Maybe one day I'll get you back

Until then, if then
Peace out

—Fee

Phillitia Charlton

Happy Father's Day

I carry your picture in my planner
So I can have you close to me
Unlike many other fathers
It was not your choice to leave me

You died before I was born
I often fantasize about what it would be like
To have a mother and a father
A nuclear family

You were not a deadbeat father
I saw a picture of you holding my sister high
Although you never got to hold me
I was blessed with your features,
Your nose, your lips and your eyes

When I look at your picture I see me
And feel that father-daughter bond
I never got to know you
But of your memory
I've grown fond

I close my eyes and ask God to give a message
From me to you
To tell you that I love you
And anything to defame your character
I would not do
I'd give anything for you to have been here

The Death of a Lie

To have been here
To teach me right from wrong
I'm hurt but I'm happy
For it is because of you that I am strong

I'll compare my mate
To the idea of the man you were
Of the man you would want him to be
Someone like you
Who watches over me in spirit
Someone who will love and take care of me

On Father's Day, I will try not to cry
This is a part of God's plan
For if you would not have died
I would not be who I am

I look to you as my protector
You keep helping me find my way
God, would you please tell my Father
I said, "Happy Father's Day!"

Phillitia Charlton

Black Hair

I am a bald-head black girl
No pigtails and ponytails
Just wigtails and phonytails
How can I be beautiful to you
When my scalp is bald and
My hair is attached with glue?
Forget you
I still think I'm fine
You can't see the bald spot
The intertwined thread is hiding
Confiding in the Korean lady
At the black beauty store
All the irony and more
Her hair is long and silky straight
A scarf is covering my coarse tangled naps
How could this longhead heffa even relate
Her hair looks like a bag number 1B
Numbers is how us weave-wearers
Distinguish color, you see
33-auburn yea that's kinda tight
Will I go Jerry Spring Curl or kinky straight
It depends on how I am feeling tonight
You want me to keep it real and raise my fist
What about my thin sides
That Blue Magic hair grease couldn't fix
Extensions and braids
Don't mean that I'm not real
Just because my original roots

The Death of a Lie

I don't want to reveal
Why do I choose to conceal
Why do I choose to surpass my inner beauty
Because I played with Barbie, Skipper,
And their cousins too
My insecurity festered
When I looked in the mirror and realized
That my hair was not blonde
And my eyes weren't blue
Examples of me were not represented
By biased toy companies
Boohoo, you too society
Fooled me to believe that my inner beauty
And nappy hair were not a reality
The concept of your reality I adopted for me
I refuse to let you define me through infinity
Release, relax, and understand beauty does not
Lye in a strand of hair
How dare you stare and compare me
To society's images
Re-image this
I am happy to be nappy or straight
My look you could not dream nor anticipate
Baldhead-fine
Weave, divine
Mind underneath
Priceless

Phillitia Charlton

Part Two:

Freshman Year

Phillitia Charlton

You and Me

Your presence immobilizes me
It creates memories of you and me
In your eyes I can see the confusion
In both you and me

Inevitably we see each other and sigh
Our conversation has been minimized
To a faint, "Hi!"

I stand motionless
I don't know what to say
All I can think of is that day
That changed anything that could ever be
Nothing is the same between you and me

The you and me I wanted us to be
Is an erased memory

You know and I can see
There will never be a you and me

Phillitia Charlton

You

I'm lonely
I'm empty
I'm confused
I'm neglected
I'm ashamed
I'm scared
I'm tired
I'm unhappy
I'm searching
I'm crying
I'm trying
I'm denying
My feelings for you

I've confessed
I've shed tears
I've stayed up all night
I've shared secrets
I've been intimate
I've been concerned
About you

I care about you
I'm open for you
Now what about me

The Light (Sweet Honey in the Rock)

In the face of fear,
In the face of strain
There comes a light through all the rain

Do you let the light in
Or do you keep it away
Or is the light so powerful
It can lead you astray

Opening your mind
Uncovering dark things
Things you could never see
Everybody has a light
It could be you
It could be me

Maybe it's not either one of us,
We just want it to be
Or maybe the light is so bright
Neither one of us can see
In the midst of the dark
What do you do
Do you try to clear your eyes
To let the light through
The light has returned as quickly as it went out
Did you want it back as fast or was there doubt
Are you happy to see
Or do you want to be blind
I guess you'll never know
Until you have an experience of each kind

Phillitia Charlton

Do You Believe?

I'm trying to learn to be alone with me
When times are hard to depend on me

I'm trying to learn not to expect love to be true
I'm trying not to classify most men like I do

I'm trying to believe there is someone for me
I'm trying to hold on to my belief in destiny

I want to believe there are rainbows
With pots of gold
I'm trying to believe I'll have a love
With whom I can grow old

As much as I want to believe
I'll tell you what I see
No one being available
Or wanting to be available to believe with me

Do you believe?

Plan B

Time on the clock goes tick tock
I'm staring at my watch
Waiting
Pacing
Thinking
Knowing he's coming to see me
Because he said he would
I know he'll be here any minute
Because he asked me if he could

Time on the clock goes tick tock
A half an hour passed
Dang
Why didn't he just call
I am standing out here waiting
It's cold out here ya'll

Wasting my time is something you need not do
I have other things on my agenda
Besides waiting for you

It's cool
While standing
While waiting
While anticipating your presence
Another man occupied my time

I'm going with him

Phillitia Charlton

Childhood Games

Will you go with me
Check no or yes
Is that the only answer
To a question you want to know
Where exactly is it that you want me to go
If I check yes
I expect the best
To be treated unparalleled
To be held in esteem above the rest
I expect you to pass my test
It's multiple choice
A, B, C, or D
It's getting complicated
Do you still want to go with me
Question one
Let's see what you want to do
When we talk about long-term commitment
What are you willing to commit to
Check A for yes
B for I'll try
C for no
You're disqualified if your percentile is too low
Are you wishing you said no
If I go with you
Can you handle a man's responsibility
If I select you we will soon see
I don't know how far I want this to go
My answer is undecided

But yet
Not no

Phillitia Charlton

Urban Hang Suite (Ode to Maxwell)

The music creeps up on me
All up and down my spine,
It fills my head
With memories
That will never fade

If I close my eyes slightly
Roll my neck
Let my head slowly sway
I can see you
Caressing the deepest part
Of my inner soul

A rhythmic funk, a seductive sweat,
A melodious tune
As our limbs relentlessly tangle themselves

Ah, the music has returned,
We are now surrounded by its infectious sound

Only you and I will ever know
Sensuous nights in an *Urban Hang Suite*
On the Hush

The Question of What Do I Want

I wanted a night's peace
I wanted you to call me saying I love you
Before I go to sleep
When you talk to me I want to hear love
In your voice
I don't want competition
I need to be the only woman of choice
When you say I'm sorry I want to believe you
I don't want to go around crying
Dwelling on the negative things
That we go through
I wanted to be close to you
I wanted to be your friend
I wanted the same amount of love
We started out with
To last from the beginning to the end
I'm in too deep
I can't sleep
Bad decisions
The penalties both you and I reap
We're holding on
Trying to keep you and I from one another
We've invested too much time
I am sick of reminiscing on a dime
About the good ole times

So what do I want?
I wanted you to love me like you used to do

Phillitia Charlton

But in the event that you didn't
And nothing has changed
Our love situation must be rearranged
Make some decisions that benefit me too

Simply put
All I wanted
Was love and respect
From you

You Couldn't Even Say Good-bye

I thought about you yesterday
I hoped you might think to call
I checked my messages
Every five minutes
Only to find nothing at all
As the time went by
I looked at the clock
A tear dropped down from my eye
I didn't even mean enough because
You couldn't say good-bye

Remember when you denied me your presence
But when you called
In your hour of need, I came
Remember when you ridiculed me
In front of my friends
I told you that you made me feel ashamed
You told me in your sincerest tone
You were not to blame
I know you didn't care if you hurt me
But I decided to give you a try
I developed feelings for you so quickly
I guess that's why it hurts
When you couldn't even say good-bye

I know your situation
But I don't understand
Why you do what you do
I guess it's not hard to play someone

Who is playing themselves
I guess I'm the fool
You told me you couldn't be with me
Your actions didn't follow your words
You can remember to call me
When you're feeling that touchy-feely urge

I don't ask for your money
Not a penny or a dime
I'm not materialistic
I'm asking for a little of your time
I guess I really want us to be together
To be you and I
But I'm the only one who feels this way
Because you couldn't even say good-bye

I know you had someone to see
She takes a higher place in your world
I know that I have no chance
And you have no intentions
Of me ever being your girl

When I first saw you
A gorgeous man
Sort of like a fantasy to me
You were caramel in color
What I would want my dream man to be
There I go again
Getting caught up in the feelings
It's a weakness I despise
Although you didn't call and say it
Your actions said good-bye

Our Time Has Passed

I know not to get used to you
Not matter how hard you try
I should have known
It was only lust
When we met eye to eye
I guess
Although I don't want to admit
Your feelings of love have passed
Let's be realistic
My decision to meet with you
Put our rotation in a lower class
Commitment doesn't fit into your life
Especially not with me
You want to be a big-time bachelor
Partying from city to city
I'm so used to getting all your time
I have to remember
You're not my man
Now, I don't get any of your time
You'll squeeze me in
If you can

Phillitia Charlton

The Final Chapter

You've answered all the questions
You've confessed your feelings
You finally let me know the truth
You broke it down and said damn girl
I couldn't care less about you

I wanted to know
I kept trying
His actions already told me
But my love for him
Caused me to keep denying
It was gone for him
But the flame was still lit for me
I felt like Lauren Hill begging you
For reciprocity

I made the mistake of showing you that I care
I made the mistake
Of getting used to you being there
I made the mistake of being young and dumb
I made the mistake of thinking
Since you were a grown man
You'd understand where I was coming from

This is the final chapter
No more pages to be flipped
I've confessed all the lines
You know the script

The Death of a Lie

You waited until I shared all my feelings
To tell me the morning after
You couldn't care less about me
This is our Final Chapter

Phillitia Charlton

New Year's Eve

I made love to a man and
Didn't know his last name
Excuse me I copulated with a man
But in my ignorance it felt just as good
It felt the same

He reminded me of what it's like
To temporarily feel good
I was so empty I need something to feel good
Like it should

I made love to a man and
Didn't know his last name
Excuse me I copulated with a man
But in my ignorance it felt just as good
It's all the same…Right?

I was alone
And loneliness and emptiness in me
Couldn't wait
I was so lonely I woke up next to a man
With whom I couldn't relate

Never took me out
We never had a date
I cooked dinner
I enjoyed his company soooooo
I cooked steak and potatoes and green beans

Some fancy dessert
Some strawberry thing
Anything to make him stay
I was lonely and empty
He was my prey

I didn't know his last name
But I wanted him to be in my presence
From tonight until the next day

I made love to a man
And didn't know his last name
Excuse me I copulated with a man
But in my ignorance it felt just as good
It's all the same

...Right?

...Right?

Phillitia Charlton

Part Three:

Sophomore Year

Phillitia Charlton

I'm Just Too Good for You

Every time I try to smile
I can count on you to make me frown
Every time I'm feeling good
You say something negative to bring me down
I'm not the prettiest
But neither are you
I'm coming to the conclusion with my time
I can find better things to do
I figured it out
You know what
I'm just too good for you.

Being in your presence
Loving when you hold me tight
But that's no longer enough
I need more than my body feeling right
If my mind is empty and my heart is raw
All the physical connecting is a lost cause
I need the sensitive tender care
returned back to me
That I give to you
I don't mean that much to you
So that's a hard task to do
You take me for granted
That's how I know
I'm just too good for you.

Phillitia Charlton

When I try
To tell you how I feel
About me and you, you say
"Yeah, baby, alright, whatever, you know we cool."
Tell me how cool you'll feel when you realize
Your phone ain't ringing and
It's not because your ringer is off
It's because I stopped calling you

Playing Brownstone's "Five Miles to Empty"
Over and over on a Friday night
Because I'm feeling blue
That's something, for my sanity,
I just can't continue to do.
I don't have to put up with this
I'll repeat it until I believe it's true

I'm just too damn good for you.

Wanting You (A Lonely College Night)

I want you to want me,
I want you to desire my mind,
My being and my time
I want you to want me with
A fierce, forceful fire in your eyes
I want you to crave me
Although I'm not in your presence
Not to be able to resist me
Grasping for my shadow
Thinking to yourself, "She is bad though"
I want you to want me so bad
You'd give your soul
To make me your woman or your girl
I want you to remember how you felt today
Ten days later
In the midnight hour
When you are doing your homework
Sitting at your desk
I want you to sit back and smile,
The image to be so real you actually feel
The sensual feeling from that night
Of my heartbeat on your chest
I want you to want to hold my hand,
That's something my heart tends to need
I want just a simple glimpse of my face
To make you quiver
Everything I say and everything I do
All end up with the fact that I want you

Phillitia Charlton

My heart is aching and my soul is blue
Pondering what can I do
To make you want me like I want you

Romance

I want a rose because you think I'm sweet
After a tired day at work
I want someone to rub my feet
I want you to put on Marvin Gaye
In the living room and ask me to dance
Simply put,
I want romance

I want to take a bath with you
No sex involved
Just a massage
As the bubbles dissolve
Put a blanket on the balcony
Let's look at the stars
Your hand in mine
We know the night is ours
All I'm asking is that you give this a chance
Simply put I need romance

A kind word to make my day
Tell me you love me
To let me know the relationship's ok
A picnic at the park
A bottle of wine
It doesn't have to be fancy
I'll pay
You don't have to spend a dime
All I need is romance
All I need is a little of your free time

Phillitia Charlton

Justification

She's not a hoe
You know
But sometimes
It's gotta go where it's gotta go
She be sayin' no, no, no
But he can tell it's yes, yes, yes
Undress
Wildness
Overdrive
Heart in cardiac arrest
Yes
No
Stop now
Please go
Hold up
Wait not yet
No not yet
Get out
No don't go
She pouts

She's not a hoe
You know
She said it out loud
Pretending to be proud

You were only supposed to be her friend
Hoe tendencies have officially kicked in

Lust, love, sin
Saying yes
This is a mess
Oh yes
Yes
No
Yes
She is sad because she gave it up
Boundaries blurred
Lines scratched up
Never had a male friend
Talks weren't enough
Never knew how to be a friend
She had it rough
But sadly
Intellectual regard wasn't enough
It still wasn't enough
Decisions of disdain
Physical pleasure
Lead to mental pain
Justified because she thinks
Only she and he will know
Rationalizing insanity
The justification of a hoe

Phillitia Charlton

What's in a Name?

Will we have relations?
Or we can call it making love.
Check box A or B or is it all of the above?

What's in a name?
I just have to ask
What's in a name
When hooking up is the task?

Darkness to erase the face
Music to replace the face
With Beyoncé or Janet Jackson

What's in a name?
When you don't even care about me
What's in a name?
When a physical conquest is all you see

You love my body, my full-sized lips
You love my small waistline
My non-injected hips

What's in a name?
Keep it real
Casual physical encounters have me numb,
Unable to feel
All that you claim we are
Tell me what's the deal?

What's in a name, it's all a game
A rose by any other name
May smell as sweet
But it's still the same

Phillitia Charlton

Double Standard

All you wanted was it
All I wanted was it too

You copped it fast
I surrendered fast
The thought of morals never came to pass

Am I now seen as a hoe
I really need to know
Now the craving is diminished
Do you want me to go?

Am I no longer the classy lady
You were attracted to
Did my willingness to participate
Surprise you

You said you wanted to do it
I replied yes

Drinks and exes make for easy yeses
Yes, that is the best
Oh, did I fail the test
Do you now view me like you view the rest?

While you are reflecting on the moment
Deciding my fate
Just remember you did willingly participate
Now what are we gonna do
Remember you didn't say no
You didn't propose that we wait
Consider that

Ponder this
It was consensual for me and you

So whatever I am
You are too

Phillitia Charlton

I Wanted So Much

I wanted so much
But I required nothing
So, that's what I got
Nothing

Part Four:

Junior Year

Phillitia Charlton

Seeking Consistency

It's the year 2000 minus 1
Putting me back in 1999
Rewind
If I could turn back the hands of time
Ever so slowly tick tock
No more hurt and make the watch stop
No more bombs of lies would drop
The pop of the Glock would not take a man out
A woman wouldn't be abused
By a man's abusive shout
It's the year 2000 minus 2
1998 junior year in school
Doin' too damn much
Doin' God knows who
Strange stuff was happening
Before D'Angelo released *Voodoo*
Don't act like it was just me
It's the year 1998 add back the 1
Nothing is consistent for me or you
Nothing is consistent upon me insisting
That you become consistent
Instead you become distant
Yet I am still consistent
And persistent
About my efforts to make you less
Resistant to a real woman
Tried and true in the new millennium
I'm ready

Phillitia Charlton

Are you ready for me
Because I'm ready for you

It's Okay

It's okay for me to be mad
That you left me when I needed you most
It's okay for me to want to shove
All the fake promises of love
Down your throat until you almost choke

It's okay for it to be two years later
And I am still pissed
It's okay for me to gag
At the thought that, once upon a time
I longed for a kiss
From your dry, chapped, ashy, lips

It's okay to be disgusted and sad
You refused to love me back
It's okay to call your home and snap
Cussing you out, daring you to talk back

It's okay for me to still be bitter,
To hate you like the KKK hates blacks
It's okay for me not to want you to die,
But to feel the severe pain of a heart attack

It's okay that I don't care
That you don't understand what sparked this
It's okay for me to think of you
As less than 0.01% of a man
Remember you started this

Phillitia Charlton

It's okay for me to know that no other woman
Will ever love you like I can
Oops, reverse that verse
I mean could,
No other woman could ever love you
Like I could

Not for Some Other Chick

5, 4, 3, 2, 1 our time is up
Our relationship is diminished
So, now what's up?

You look me in the eyes,
And tell me in your sincerest tone
You've learned a lot from me
And how much you've grown

You say I taught you how to love,
Show respect, display honesty, but
Our relationship is over
So, how does your newfound knowledge benefit me

Well I'm glad you're happy
You have new insight on relationships,
And how to feel bliss
But I didn't teach you that stuff to share
With some other chick

You told me you learned,
That having money isn't everything
You told me you never experienced
A love so strong,
And one day you wanted me to wear your ring

I took you out to dinner and filled up your tank,
I bought you nice things

Phillitia Charlton

I guess you changed your mind
After you graduated from school
As long as you were broke
Our relationship was cool

I stood by your side when you were poor,
But now that you've found your niche
You dumped me,
To get with some other chick

Stupid

You must think I'm stupid
Idiotic dumb and blind,
If you believe that I believe
You didn't do it this time
You done lost your mind
I'm losing mine too
The stuff you got for me
I don't want to go through.

You telling me it wasn't you I saw
Holding hands with her
Walking through the mall
That dating service my friend called
She said she heard your voice
Description and all
I hit redial
I heard it too
Negro I know your voice,
Don't say it wasn't you

You must think I'm stupid
Idiotic dumb and blind,
If you believe that I believe
You didn't do it this time.
You done lost your mind
I'm losing mine too
The stuff you got for me
I don't want to go through.

Phillitia Charlton

Cheers to Me

I got a job
I need a man
I need to get back in school, as fast as I can.
I have a two-bedroom apartment
With a roommate.
The chick is broke and her child stank
She can't pay rent and if she does pay rent, it's late
I feel as if I've been bamboozled, hoodwinked
And even led astray
I'm not as strong as Malcolm X
So I am not going to be ok
I just lost my job today
Boss said I was rude,
Said I had a nasty attitude
Now I'm screwed
And, if Amy from Discover calls me
One more freakin' time
Hell, I wish she would,
I'd cuss her white bubbly behind out,
Talkin' 'bout are you gonna pay,
I'd say chick, hell nah
I just lost my freakin' job today.
You know the part-time man I'm with
He has started to clown
Says he has a child and
Probably a wife and girlfriend to match
You know his behind lied
And didn't tell me he was a horrible catch

The Death of a Lie

I'm gonna throw his behind back in the sea,
Bound and gagged
With a 5000lb weight on his neck to make sure
He drowns
But it's okay, sweetie
I'm going to be okay
I'm a strong black woman
I can take it.
Although I'm down
I'll get back up,
So cheers to me everybody
Raise up your cup

Phillitia Charlton

He Got Me Messed Up

That's it,
I quit,
You got me messed up
You know like a scorned woman once said,
"If that Negro don't start calling I'm gonna
Bust him upside his head!"

That's it,
I quit,
You got me messed up
You know like a scorned woman once said,
"If he makes one more foolish comment,
I'm going to get very mad!"

That's it,
I quit,
You got me messed up
I know I said it before,
But ya'll I'm hurting
So I'm going to say it
Until I can't say it no more.

That's it,
I quit
You got me messed up
It's 3:00 am on a Saturday night
Oh, now you want to call and
Get some, well Negro,

Your game ain't that tight!

That's it,
I quit,
You got me messed up
This is my last time saying it for real.
Although I'm mad,
Maybe he's for real,
He was probably just busy
Earlier in the day.
Even if it is 3:00 am in the morning
Maybe we'll just talk
He'll see things my way.

That's it,
I quit
You got me messed up
You caught me
I said it again, yea I lied.
Ya'll I'm falling for this dumb man's game
My hands are tied.

Then I thought about it
I woke up and stopped dreamin'
At 3:00am in the morning he just wants some
Who in the world does he think he's schemin'.

Well since he's not getting a piece and
I'm not getting my way
I guess I'll just go to sleep
Maybe tomorrow will be a better day.

Phillitia Charlton

Dumb Chick

Either he has a job and a woman
Or he don't have anything to work with.
If he has a job without a woman
He got screwed in the head
By some dumb chick.
Who are you dumb chick
So I can whip your behind
For poisoning all the good men's brains.
What are you doing to all these brotha's
That causes them to think
To love a woman is insane,
And can only lead to pain?
He doesn't trust me because of you,
He doesn't believe the love
Of a woman can ever be true.
He holds back his feelings
When I try to get inside his head
When I tell him I love him,
He doesn't believe a word I've said.
You mess up men's brains,
I guess that's your niche
Thanks for nothing,

Dumb Chick

Bitter

You say my poems are bitter
You wonder why I write the way I do
If you had dealt with
Half the stuff I've dealt with
You'd be bitter too

Grab a pencil and a pen
I am about to take you to my school...

I had a man call talking 'bout
"Can we go to the hotel today?"
Where did all this money come from
Because you couldn't even buy me
A 99-cent value meal yesterday

You have enough money
To go to the hotel with
But you can't find money any other day
Step off
Get out of my face
You're putting me in
Bitter black girl mode today

You see it's not me
I'm not personally bitter
Some people made me this way
My words are wrath
My pen is my fuel

Phillitia Charlton

To help me make it through the day

Now
One more thing before I go
To help you further understand
See I'm a single black woman
You know
The kind without a man

I guess you look at me now and say
"Oh, now I see
That girl is bitter because
She is mean and lonely."

One day I'll write about stars
And all the joy that love can bring
One day I'll write about flowers
And the birds that can sing
But for now
I'm not feeling it
So I am going to write about what I know
I am lonely and I am bitter
If you can change it
Let me know

Now, I am not going to lower my standards
So come correct or don't come at all
I'm lonely but I'm not desperate
That is something you need to know
Don't play with my heart or my feelings or
You'll put me back in bitter black girl mode

See What Had Happened Was...

If a man starts a sentence off with
"See what had happened was my boy...."
You automatically know he is telling a lie
Tell the Negro to take a time out in the corner
Give his lie another try

The umms and rambling over words
Already give his lying behind away
You just asked him where he was
He's at a loss for words,
He can't find a thing to say

You ain't sorry 'cause you black
You sorry because of how you act
And you actin' ignorant and playing dumb
To what other conclusion
Was I supposed to come?

I pulled your hoe card, called you out,
Oh now you mad, now you gonna shout?
Oh, so I'm acting like
The word that rhymes with witch
That's funny,
That's what I was about to call you,
You're the one throwing a tantrum
Like a two-year-old fool.

You'd better call Jerome and tell him come on,

Phillitia Charlton

Because I know you're about to get
Your broke behind out of my home
Now you're sorry it went this far,
You say no baby for real I was chillin'
With my boys at the bar.

You still have to go,
But if that was all it was
Why didn't you just let me know
All that's well and good, but remember,
Didn't you call me that word
That rhymed with witch?

Get to steppin',
I might let you call me back
When you're done throwing hissy fits!

Trophy

Opening myself to let you in
Quietly pleading for you
To want to be more than my friend

Giving my body continuously
Always available relentlessly
Surrendering to all my curiosity
But when it's time for commitment
You run from me

You don't want me
To be with anyone else
Yet you don't want me for yourself
Telling your friends that I belong to you
Claiming me like property
Making me feel like a fool

I am an actress for you
On a scale of one to ten
My performance is an eleven
Ignoring my own truth
The pain of us
Takes me to my knees
Praying to God in Heaven

You take me out of the closet
Only for company to see
When everyone leaves to go home
You're finished with me

I don't find it a privilege
To be used as your trophy.

Phillitia Charlton

Priceless

I am priceless
I am a rare jewel,
A precious gem
A diamond in the rough
Men that have been privileged
To encounter me can't get enough
What I have here is like no other
It is truly the best
Ask any of my ex-lovers and they will tell you
I am priceless

Donald Trump or Bill Gates
Couldn't put a down payment on this
MC Hammer said it perfectly when he said,
"You can't touch this."
Call me vain, call me crude,
But I'm just stating the facts
I can't help it if I am addictive
Like a junkie feenin' for crack
What I have here defeats monetary value
It's better than what you thought was the best
If you didn't know,
I am priceless

There's no other way to define me,
My aroma is so sweet
I possess a potent aphrodisiac
Immaculate, impeccable

Mind and essence very much intact

Feel it in your ventricles
Original
Exceptional
I am more precious than the rest
If you were privileged enough
To garner my attention
To present me with your best
You would have known that I was priceless

In a second's time
Grace and beauty combined
Divine plan accomplished, mission outlined
I am priceless
Bask in silence

Phillitia Charlton

I Used to Have a Friend

My girl
My homie
My ace
Our bond was tight
Our friendship no one could ever replace
I used to have a friend

You need me
I'm there
Your man is tripping
I'm listening
Girl you know I care
It's four am in the morning
I swear
Forget it I'm coming
I'll be right there
I used to have a friend

Have you ever had a friend
Who used to be true
You would make sacrifices
For each other
That's what real friends do
Then all of a sudden
She changed
She got a man
He was her new best friend
Her life was rearranged

The Death of a Lie

Your relationship has demised
She was just an angel in disguise

Let me put a bug in your ear
Give a note to the wise
You can tell I'm sincere
By the tears in my eyes
Give a (wo)man an inch
She will take a yard
Losing who you thought
Would be your best friend for life
Is hard

Phillitia Charlton

Watch Out:
A Conversation Amongst Friends

You trust him, don't believe him
Don't believe him
What he says ain't true
Remember what he did to that one girl
Girl, he will do the same to you

I know I ain't got a man
He ain't never gonna ever
Put me through that stuff
All he is doing is making your life unbearable
Making your life rough
I'm telling you girl,
I'm your friend I know
Have you heard the rumor that
He's a community property hoe

All men are dogs
Your man, humph, he ain't worth it
What, girl, he said he loves you
You betta quit

I saw him last night kickin' it at the club
Girl, if I were you I'd watch him
He was freaking all the ladies down and up

Girl, you don't want to be with him anymore

The Death of a Lie

I'm glad you realized he's not your type
As soon as she hung up I called him
Asked him was it on again for tonight

She's my friend and I love her,
But, her man is right for me
I'm glad I convinced her to leave him
So he and I can be together
Like it's supposed to be

I know y'all think I'm scandalous
But damn her man,
Excuse me, my man is fine
Anyway if she was doing
What she was supposed to be doing
It wouldn't have been that easy
To make him mine

Oh well, one woman's lost,
Another woman's gain
That's what she gets for taking my advice
And not listening to her man

Phillitia Charlton

A Letter Never Mailed

Why, why did you never call back?
I thought everything was alright
And when you wouldn't leave to go home
I knew everything flowed right

Well you had me fooled for a minute
You run a good game
Although you cheated me
After five minutes
You selfishly
Couldn't keep your excitement tamed

Humph, if anyone stopped calling
It should have been me
But my lonely eyes would not allow me to see
That you were not worthy enough to be a part of my
destiny

It hurts like hell and I don't understand
See I had plans of dealing with a real man
But obviously you couldn't relate
Because you still chose to violate
The space I allowed you to have
With no intentions to stay
Even though I'm not on your mind
I still think of your sorry self today

You'll never get this letter

The Death of a Lie

Because you don't deserve to know
I feel as though you played me like a hoe
You hit it, quit it, stepped on my emotions
And slammed the door

See I like closure in my life
But I guess that's too much to ask
Because you couldn't even complete
The simple task
Of telling me all you wanted to do
Was tap me fast

You call yourself a real man,
Well, I disagree
'Cause a real man would have enough guts
To say all he wanted to do is screw me!

Truly Yours

Phillitia Charlton

Part Five:

Senior Year

Phillitia Charlton

The Vibe

Tonight
I guess you want me
To stand in front of you
With words to make you say ooh
To talk about relationships and
Who made me feel blue
You're anticipating here
What I will do tonight
Well the vibe in here
It isn't quite right

You want to hear me curse
You want to hear me say
Sugar honey ice tea
Or you want to giggle
Because I referred
To the plight of the relationships
Over enunciating with efficacy

You want me to share my world
Hear what I have to say
You want to misinterpret my poems
See them your way
Well, surprise
Not tonight
The vibe in here isn't quite right

You want to give me a high-five

Phillitia Charlton

Congratulate me and say
"Girl, your poem was tight"
Or you want to stare at me
In confusion
When you have never written
A thing in your life,
I could share what I write
That things were alright
Well tonight you won't have the opportunity
Tonight is just not your night
I'm not feelin' y'all
I'm telling you
The vibe in here ain't right

I'm starting to like this
Not telling you about me
Maybe you can relate to another poem,
But this one is especially written for me
I don't care if you're not inspired or
If you think I'm rude
Maybe you're right
Maybe I do have an attitude
I'm sorry
I will read you a poem tonight

Nah
I'm just playing
I told you the vibe in here isn't quite right

A Plea

Tiny ropes connected to each limb
Pulling at my soul,
All paths have road closed signs,
This situation is beyond my control.
Nowhere to run to, nowhere to hide
Such disarray is taking a toll on my pride.
So many different opinions
As to what I should do.

My mental status is messed up,
I might withdraw from school.
Will you please help me
Regain the structure in my life?
Will you please help me
Help a young black sistah
Because the ropes are getting tight!

I'm crying inside,
My failure I can't deny,
My path is bleak, my future seems obsolete,
This is my final plea,
Can you please help me?
Release the ropes that are tearing at my soul,
Release the chains, I'm losing control!
I'm looking to you as mortal as me,
The answer lies in a source
Beyond what we are able to see,

Phillitia Charlton

So I'll change my plea
Get down on my knees and ask the Lord,
"Hey, Lord, can You please help me?"

Acronyms

You've been burned by desire
You've been burned, but not by fire
Your burn did not leave
Your skin black and blue
It left a scar in the form of a lesion or two

At your daily trip to the doctor's office
When he whispers in your ear
He wants to make his message crystal clear
Acronyms are nothing
You want or desire to hear
He's mumbling something about
STD, HIV, AID, PID
W
A
R
T
S
All results from your need to practice
Unprotected sex

Here's a simple equation
Stay with me on this
We don't have a condom
Forget it
Let's do it
We both agree to use the pull-out method
So screw it

Equals a poor unhealthy,
Unwanted fetus
Floating around
In toxic fluid
You've been burned by desire
You've been burned, but not by fire
All for the sake of I-T it
It ain't worth it
A little latex
Some self-love and self-respect
Some protected sex
Will keep your body from the
STD, HIV, AID, PID
Acronym path

Excuses

Sky-high
Sky-high
Sky-high
Until the day you die
Take another puff, brother
Keep getting high
Become a slave to weed
Which you say isn't a drug
Keep sagging your pants
Be true to the title called "Thug"

Keep following the path
Keep killing brothers in a violent wrath
Fight over a food tray
When y'all are both slowly dying
In the jailhouse café

Remain a N-I-G-G-A
Keep getting high
Keep smoking weed daily
Keep collecting your pay
From a brother or sister
You strung out on crack, cocaine, heroin
Or ecstasy yesterday
Rep your hood, my nigga
Tell 'em it's all good, my nigga
Wish they would, my nigga

Phillitia Charlton

Let them know
You from the Midwest, my nigga
You quick to pull the trigger
On anotha' nigga
Well...
You don't own any land
You don't have government contracts
Or blue prints
You have never seen a real estate plan
None of the property belongs to you
But you the man, right
Or are you the fool?

I know you saying
You gotta do what you gotta do
The white man is out to get you
It is not the man you are running from
You are running away from you
And other messed up men
Who have the same mentality as you do

Scared

Everyone I get close to tends to shy away
I'm scared to get close to you
What if you don't stay

It scares me when I think of you
Every time I turnaround,
It scares me when I hear your voice
How fast my heart begins to pound

It scares me how I long to get next to you
I miss you until the next time we get in touch
It scares me that
You are on my mind this much

I'm scared that you will get tired,
Not want to hear my voice anymore
Like everyone else
You will quickly close your door
Keeping me out, not allowing me to see
Whether or not it was you
Who was truly my destiny

It scares me how you might realize
You really just want to be my friend
It scares me how
Any day you could bring this to an end

It scares me that my soul

Phillitia Charlton

Can't get enough of you
It scares me that anything you ask
I am more than willing to do
In all the scariness and all the fear
My heart is the key
My heart is aching to have you near
While you're near
I'll whisper in your ear
Although I'm scared
I'm glad you're here

It Just Is

What is right?
What is wrong?
What isn't right is wrong, right?
Left field is the place where your lie resides
It's not the truth
You show it in your eyes
I know the difference
Between right and wrong
As long as I'm always right. Wrong!

Left
Right
Right
Left
Right
Wrong
Right
Left
Wrong
Right, go the thoughts in your mind
Constantly trying
I am confusing you right, wrong!
You're not listening to my poem right!
Or could I be wrong for going
On and on and on
Presenting this information
A little too long
I thought I was right,

But I guess I was wrong,
Right?
You can be right and still be wrong.

Opinions

Should I?
Shouldn't I?
It's all up to me
My decisions affect my fate
Ultimately, it's my responsibility
Who are you to tell me what to do?
I have enough on my mind
Than to worry about your opinion

Since when do you think
That it is going to help me
To hear what you have to say
No matter what
It only affects my day today
And every other day

I am up against a wall so high
Like Mary Mac Mac Mac
It touched the sky sky sky

I am climbing this wall
Trying to find...Me

Phillitia Charlton

To My Seed

Forgive your father
For he knows not what he has done
Regardless of my lack of consent, it happened
He has forgotten
It took two of us to bring you into this world
Not just one

To my beautiful seed
Heart beating inside my soul
Essence more precious
Than any amount of platinum
Silver or gold

I pray everyday
For your health and your mind
I pray every day that you are strong
In a world that can be so unkind

I pray to teach you all things I never learned
I pray your respect is something
I will be able to earn
To my seed
Four and a half months in the making
Everything inside of me is yours for the taking

I am not embarrassed but proud to claim you
Any man that doesn't want you
Doesn't want me

The Death of a Lie

Any man who loves me will see
That being your mommy is my first priority

Although your father is not around
God is by our side
He blessed me with your beautiful seed
So
Still I rise
And hold my head up high with pride

To my seed
Just the two of us
We can make it
We have to try
No, just the three of us
You,
God
And I

Phillitia Charlton

I Wait - A Choral Poem

I get so lonely
I cannot sleep
I pray my soul
My soul He'll keep
I've been wrong
But I'm trying to do right
So I'll sleep alone
Alone tonight

I'm gonna wait
Til the midnight hour
Until my Savior calls
I'm gonna wait
Til the midnight hour
Until God brings him home

I'm gonna wait
Til the midnight hour
Until my Savior calls
I'm gonna wait
Til the midnight hour
Until God brings him home

I'm on my knees in my mind
Trying to find my purpose in life
Receive what God has intended for me,
But lust and worldly sin won't let me be
It rides my back

The Death of a Lie

You know, like
A girl in one of those bad movies

Lord, it's a struggle
In this life
Constant turmoil, strife
Every day
I go from low to high, I wonder why
It makes me want to die, not try
I cannot continue
Living this way
Sounds familiar
As I press replay everyday

I'm feeling it though
'Cause I want to be free
Completely free
Allow others to see past my physical
And enter my realm of intellectual reality
Where weakness of the flesh no longer exists
And my intelligence holds attention
That no good man could resist

It stings, the emotional blows
I hit myself with when I step away
From my path and ignore my goals
In time I'm frozen
The world moves on
And I stand still
Waiting, waiting, waiting
For God to send me what I need

But Satan tries to make me believe
That since I don't want to give it up
I'm stuck alone to raise my seed,
That without a man
I won't be able
To give my daughter what she needs
But I see through it,
His divine light shines through it
Tranquility prevails and peace enters my mind
I realize that it is in his time not mine
Lord, release me
From this negative mind state
Reveal me to my soul mate
Allow me to see
That every man that enters my life
You did not send to me
Keep me on the path
Help me to walk straight
Until you are ready
Lord, I wait.

I get so lonely
I cannot sleep
I pray my soul
My soul He'll keep
I've been wrong
But I'm trying to do right
So I'll sleep alone
Alone tonight

I'm gonna wait
Til the midnight hour
Until my Savior calls
I am gonna wait
Til the midnight hour
Until God brings him home

I'm gonna wait
Til the midnight hour
Until my Savior calls
I am gonna wait
Til the midnight hour
Until God brings him home

Phillitia Charlton

Happiness

I'm Smiling
I'm Laughing
I'm Chuckling
I'm Giggling
Thinking of you and that voodoo that you do to me
My brain is insane
With thoughts of Jazz,
Blues
And Saxophones too...oooh!
Does it get any better than this melodious bliss
Of sounds compounded into a beautiful song
So strong is the music in my ear
To my lips
In route to my breasts
Then

D
  o
    w
      n
         M
           y
              S
                p
                  i
              n
            e

Back up my nose
Through my toes
Who knew that music had the power
To do what no man has ever done
Music makes me come alive

Phillitia Charlton

Part Six:

Short Story & A Long Prose

Phillitia Charlton

To Anyone Who is Listening

I never thought it would be me, that's why I was mortified when I read the article. I mean, what type of woman or person could do what she did? Oh, and the way she did it! What type of mindset do you have to be in to be so desperate and downright evil? I mean, you make it all the way to college on scholarship and then, you do that? What an oxymoron! To be in a place that fosters free thought, problem solving and critical thinking and all you can come up with is what she did. I am usually not one to read the newspaper but this article effortlessly caught my attention. When I saw it on the table, I grabbed it and began to read.

Fetus and trash can are seldom words seen on the front page of a newspaper, let alone a newspaper in the Bible Belt of the south, otherwise known as Montgomery, Alabama. The local newspaper headline read: *Fetus found in a trash can outside a local college.* As I read it, I tried to remember her face. I tried to conjure up any interaction or experiences the girl and I in the article might have had. I imagined her as an ambitious girl. A go-getter from a small southern town not too far from campus. I believe she was excited when she got accepted into college. I imagine her parents were proud of their little girl. The article stated she was an honor student and lived in the dorms. The editor went on to say that her world was turned upside down when she found out that she was pregnant. A few months later the innocent college student was escorted out of the dorm by the state police. I heard people say that her face was welted with tears, and her head hung low from shame as she was driven away from her bright future to face the consequences of her actions. The honor student, at my alma mater, had taken the life of her unborn child. The article had all the gruesome details. A wire hanger, trash bag and bleach were the tools she used for the self-inflicted pain. The hanger could not remove the pain she felt inside; a black plastic trash bag could not cover or smother the memories of the baby. The bleach might temporarily conceal the attempts to wipe away the blood, but bleach could by no means cover up the permanent stains left on her soul, forever. As I placed the article back on the table in the dorm recreation lounge, I asked myself why. Why? What mindset was she in to harm a newborn baby as well as mutilate herself? Was her narrow view of the world so close-minded that this was the only option she thought she had? I don't know. I do know we need to provide atmospheres where women can feel comfortable talking with someone, anyone, about being pregnant....

Two Lines

Two lines.

"Don't two lines mean you're pregnant?" I mumbled. *This can't be right*, I thought. The second line looked slightly faded. I looked through the thinly folded accordion-like instructions to see if two lines actually meant the test was positive.

"Two lines," I said more audibly. I searched to see if the instructions said anything about a faded second line. There is no way that all these boxed tests, shipped from India or China, were all accurate. The test clearly had to be wrong. I couldn't and refused to believe it was positive. That day, I took three tests. All the tests I took came back with two lines. I never missed a period until that one. I was so tired. I was sleepy all the time and moody as hell. I was officially pregnant.

Hook, Line and Sinker

We were riding back from our fishing trip. We didn't get to see each other a lot so this was a great opportunity to rekindle our long distance relationship. His college friends rented an RV near Lake Michigan for fall break. When he asked me to join him, I was so excited. I'd never been fishing. My excitement dulled as I was forced with the decision of when to tell him I was pregnant. It was too late to cancel and I knew it was the right thing to do. I had to tell him. During the trip, we took a boat out to sail and I could hardly stand. I was woozy and dizzy. He thought I was sea sick, and I went along with it. I knew that wasn't the time to tell him, but I would have to soon; besides, I already scheduled my appointment. I had to get ready to face him and my truth. I decided I would do it on the way back home. We were riding back home and I started to probe his brain. You know, asking questions like, "If I ever got pregnant would you want me to keep the baby?"

He responded with a low unconvincing, "Yes."

I convinced myself that it didn't matter what he said because my mind was already made up. I adjusted my seat and slightly turned to face him. I slouched and said, "Guess what. I'm pregnant."

When he realized he was swerving into the median, he quickly regained control of the car and replied, "Huh?"

It shocked me that I told him because for a while I contemplated only telling my closest friend.

With a look of disbelief he asked, "What are you going to do?

As the tears formed in my eyes, I lowered my head and told him that I wasn't ready to have a baby.

He told me that whatever decision I made, I had his support.

As much as I wanted to believe him, I could sense the relief flowing through him as I released him from the possible duties of the long-term responsibilities of fatherhood.

The Attic

When he dropped me off at home, my head was spinning. Thoughts of insecurity, rejection and fear whirled in my mind like a category five tornado. I knew better. I used protection. Okay, I used protection most of the time.

How are people going to look at me? How was I going to live with myself? Abortion is wrong. Could I still go to heaven? What about school? What about my scholarship?

"My great aunt is going to kill me," I said in an incomprehensible voice. The semester had come to a screeching halt as soon as I determined my fate. I was scared to tell my friends. I was scared to face the unwanted opinions and the "If it were me I would" statements. I just wanted to be left alone. I wanted to wake up from this nightmare. I wanted to return back to the innocent reality I once enjoyed; a reality vibrant with summer vacations, full of bright sunny skies, fun cookouts in the park and sandy beaches.

This summer I spent the majority of my time in my bedroom at home. My room was in the attic. My room possessed the information I received from the doctor's office, the procedures to follow for women seeking to have an abortion and the location of the clinics. My room in the attic hid the conversations between me and my boyfriend. The room in the attic hid "the situation" from my great aunt, who was my guardian. My room also hid the tears that were wiped away before going downstairs to join my aunt and sister for dinner. My room in the attic allowed me an attempt at the peace and tranquility that I needed to think. I just needed to breathe. I could breathe up there. I just needed a minute to regain the inner strength that was slowly, but unfailingly, fading away.

D-Day

As the day approached for the abortion to take place, my nerves were up and my spirits were down. Before I got pregnant, I thought it (being pregnant without being married) only happened to "those girls". You know those girls who were promiscuous or fast; the project girls, the hoodrats, the hoochies, or anyone else but me. I was a smart, intelligent young woman in college on an academic scholarship and I was focused on the future. I mean, I kicked it, but I was definitely not one of "those girls" or at least that's what I told myself. My false self-perception wasn't enough to exempt me from becoming pregnant.

Upon approaching the clinic with my friend, who didn't want to be there, several protesters—locked and loaded with Bibles and anti-abortion signs in hand—marched. One protestor was dressed in an all-black cloak. He looked like he had dark, black, deep-set eyes like the grim reaper. The reaper even had a scythe. A scythe is the tool the Grim Reaper carries to collect or reap the souls of the dead. The demonstrators tried to give me pamphlets with graphic pictures of embryos and partially developed fetuses. They tried to tell me that I had other options. The anti-abortion activists shouted and pleaded telling me that the Lord would not forgive me. I took a deep breath, as tears spilled down my cheeks and continued my walk of shame.

When I walked through the door, I was half-heartily greeted by a security guard in a bulletproof vest. He asked for ID from my friend and me when we checked in. Then, he checked our purses. Once inside the clinic, my friend sat sullenly in the waiting room. I gave her a long gaze and entered the hallway leading to the dreaded holding room.

Only women getting an abortion were permitted in the sequestered holding room area. The holding room was eerily open, leaving all of us sitting there exposed. We all witnessed each other experiencing something private that was now public. There were no partitions or dividers in the holding room. As we sat there waiting for our turn, we couldn't hide from each other. We couldn't hide from ourselves. The silence grew louder and more awkward. The need to explain, connect or release seemed to arise in all of us. I don't know who went first or how it happened, but we began to talk. We shakenly shared our stories of the journey and decisions that got us to this point. There I met a thirteen-year-old girl and a married woman. The thirteen-year-old girl and her mother decided that she was too young to have a baby. The married woman decided, along with her husband, that they could not afford another child. Then, there was me; a nineteen-year-old college student still trying to succeed in life. There I sat as a foster girl who beat the odds and earned a college scholarship. I was the child of a drug addicted crack head mother and I worked hard not to become another African-American statistic. At the clinic, our ages and situations were different, but our purpose was the same—we all decided to have an abortion.

Even though I was smart, it still happened. Even though I knew better, I still got pregnant. Even though this guy actually liked me, he didn't try to stop me. If I'm being honest with myself, he couldn't stop me. There, at the clinic, at that moment, nothing resonated but the painstaking shame. Although my friend physically brought me to the abortion clinic, she was not really emotionally there for me. She didn't know how to be. She had her own demons to deal with. She kept trying to get pregnant. Her pregnancies were never successful. My friend wanted a baby so badly but she kept having miscarriages. And I, her best friend, could actually have a baby and I was aborting it. There was really no one there for me because I didn't feel as though I could let anyone in. I let the fear of people's opinions shut me out from the support that I so urgently needed. I didn't consider myself a church girl but from my upbringing I knew of God and I knew I needed Him to get through this. When I was in church, I remember hearing this Scripture:

> "Let anyone of you who is without sin be
> the first to throw a stone at her."
> —John 8:7 NIV

I was her. If people are religious then they of all people know none of us are walking around the earth without sin. Who is to say that one person's sin is greater or lesser than mine in the eyes of the Lord? My experience was a humbling experience. I used to be so judgmental and now it was my turn. I am not only more empathetic to women who are going through this experience, but I know by sharing my story, I can help women heal and understand that they are not alone. Just the words, "I am here for you", could keep babies out of trash cans and dumpsters, and prevent women from acts of self-mutilation. I do not believe in abortion as a means of birth control. This story is not meant to encourage abortions. That is something I will never ever do again, regardless of the situation. When a woman knows that she can't handle the responsibility of a child, then she should make the choice that she believes is best for her life, her spirit and her heart. This experience is mine, but it is one of which I am no longer ashamed. I have prayed for forgiveness. I know there is a lesson to be learned in every experience, when you face it. I believe by telling the truth and not hiding this ordeal, someone might be less ashamed. Someone might be able to heal if they know that they are not the only one, even though it might seem that way. I might convince someone's girlfriend, daughter, wife, or teenager to talk to one person who will convince them not to have an abortion. To anyone who is listening or aches to be heard, I offer my journey and my heart, but most of all, I offer my empathy and understanding.

Phillitia Charlton

The Demise of the Westside

Between concrete buildings
And cracked sidewalks
Lies hurt and despair
Broken dreams, peeled ceiling, stained carpets,
Leaky faucets not repaired.
Shattered dreams, splattered hearts,
Linty plaits, tattered clothes, blank stares
Hurt and pain shut inside
Are the symptoms of the disease called
The demise of the Westside.

Mom and pop stores boarded up
Cracked glass in windows that no longer sees
Happy nappy children playing hopscotch
Drawn with the big chalk,
Played with a big rock
That came from the cracked sidewalk
Because the foundation wasn't too good,
No more reflections in the glass,
Just tall grass, surrounded by weeds
Boarded up by the police.
The building has secrets now
Of what it witnesses on the streets,
Kids' unsupervised,
Home ownership down,
Rental property high,
Key components that lead
To the demise of the Westside.

Empty industrial buildings
No longer the mecca of the city
Outsourced to China,
Children have to say bye now
To the home in foreclosure
Because daddy didn't get his degree,
His hands were always enough to feed his kids
With a little extra too,
Damn if he had only went back to school,
But he didn't
Because he was loyal to the company,
Now the eviction notice
Taped to the screen door
Brought tears to a grown man's eyes.
Can someone write a prescription
To heal this affliction known as
The demise of the Westside?

Mental illness penetrates the veins
And spills out of the mouths of the
Misunderstood homeless,
The promiscuous teenage girl
Who's been through the block,
The mother of the suffocated baby
Serving time,
The uncle that tells his nieces to keep secrets,
The aunt who beats the nieces if they repeat it,
Between concrete buildings
And cracked sidewalks
These buried stories hide.
Is there a prescription

To heal the affliction called
The demise of the Westside?

The place where poverty is worshipped
Like a false god
And the sacrifice is
The soul of the youth
Seeping through the pores of a nation
Phenomenon,
Minds far gone,
No love for nappy-headed hoes,
Gigs, skanks, b plus itches,
Just love for snitches,
Even if it means
Protecting a rapist, murderer,
Molester, or killer,
Even if it's the drug dealer
Who turned your sister into a crack head
Who is now dead,
Your memory turns blank
All because of a street code
That has no room for accountability
No bulletproof vest for the babies
Caught in the middle of misled men
Representing a block of projects
Owned by the government
Brought about as an experiment
Where wars take place
Between concrete buildings
And cracked sidewalks.
This is not a game, this is real talk,

A synonym that should be an antonym
To this unrelenting, harsh, severe depiction
That is labeled with an unfilled prescription
As we beg for the cure with our weeping eyes
To the disease known as
The demise of the Westside.

Phillitia Charlton

I Refuse to Apologize for being a Strong, Black Woman in the 21st Century

I will not apologize because
I am not a public headscarf
Downtrodden, house-shoe wearing,
Oppressed, stressed depressed black woman

I will not succumb to the stereotype,
I am not a money-hungry
Silicone-injected
Amorous black woman
Growing up solely seeking
To become a dope boy's trap house wife

I take pride in my appearance
My mere presence demands respect
My aurora commands it
My God said I am the salt of the earth,
Why would you expect me to be bland, then?

I will not explain why my hair is natural
Nor will I question you
Because your hair is straight or straightened
How does that even begin to connect
To our intelligence the two are simply not related

I will not accept your label of militant
Because I bring out the beauty in my all of my black
I will not be defined by your futile attack
And lack of understanding

Of how I got the dip
In the very small of my back

In a board meeting, in the pulpit
Or just walking down the street
You are viewing the essence of what God made
From the top of my head to the soles of my feet
Question Him if you wonder why
He chose to make me discrete

I refuse to apologize for being a strong black woman
In the 21st century to justify your intimidation of me
I was born this way,
So that's good for some
But for me that's not okay

I will not apologize when I get excited
Or for the resonance and inflection in my voice
Not being docile does not make me ghetto
These are my expressions of choice

I will not apologize because
I get passionate when I speak
I will not apologize because
Me, being a strong black woman,
Should not make you feel weak

I refuse to apologize for being a strong black woman
In the 21st century

I will not apologize for the way
My red clay Georgia soil
Forms and pours into a pair of 4-inch heels,
I frankly will not apologize at all

I will not remove my heels
From my statuesque figure
Because you feel unequivocally short
While I stand peacock tall

I am comprised from the dreams
Of the souls of my ancestors
Who could not imagine a day they'd be free,
I conscientiously, boldly, powerfully
Stand for them and for me

I do apologize for some things
Because for a while I was misled
I got it wrong
I glamorized my features
And paraded them on display
Not aware of the stereotype I represented
Ignorant and dismayed
Sarah Baartman did that for me
She paid the ultimate price
Being publicly humiliated sexually sold

A huge part of African-American history
A story about the black women's
Public perception seldom told
This woman was taken from our country
Paraded around Europe
As some sort of circus freak
When she was a beautiful person
With a soul I pray my Lord to keep
Being objectified
Because the shape of her body

Was something they had never seen
Minimized by her original beauty
She was a true fallen African Queen

I refuse to apologize for being a strong black woman
In the 21st century

Acknowledging the attempt to dismantle
Yet constantly emulate
Confusing young black women
Into trying to become something they are
Made on purpose
As uniquely crafted
Tailor built
Like the illuminating sumptuous North Star

It's a surprise to some
Unfamiliar with the Creator's master plan
To architect a black being so beautiful
And unique no man could understand
The fullness of hips, the tightly coiled hair
The plump lips
Embody a conduit, expelling shuddering breaths
Often to defend, define or explain the unexplainable
To irrational people who lack depth

We must preach and teach and scream and cry
We must let black and brown girls
And women be assured
We are charged to never give up and to always try
As our beautiful first lady Michelle Obama
Our forever FLOTUS said,
"When they go, low we high."

Phillitia Charlton

Remaining intact
Demonstrating tact
Being kinder to each other
Not putting the knife in another black woman's back

I refuse to apologize for being a strong black woman
In the 21st century

I most certainly will not
I will celebrate other black women
Monolithic we are not
We are fabulous
We slay
We are so tough they know by our look
That says we don't play

We are record-breaking
History-making
Risk-taking
Grandma put her foot in it dinner-making
Double take neck-breaking
Monumental contributions to society
Merely earth-shaking
With the understanding that this world
This world is better because of us...
Your revelation, if you're not one of us...
Pain-staking...

When we step into our calling
We don't step we glide,
Our resilience awakening
Eradicating every single barrier
Everything in our vision is ours for the taking

About Phillitia Charlton

From foster care to becoming the first principal of a dropout recovery alternative school to being named a National Urban School of Excellence before age 40, Phillitia (phill-lee-thee-au) Charlton has always been resilient and determined to make every moment count. Phillitia's Christian faith along with her fundamental approach to facing and embracing her past is a message of deliverance. *The Death of a Lie* poetry collection is her honest and open poetic college diary that conveys the important message that making mistakes does not make you a mistake.

While only 2% of children formerly in foster care earn a bachelor's degree or higher, Phillitia has exceeded the odds by completing multiple graduate-level programs. She has a Bachelor of Arts Degree in Public Relations and a Master of Arts Degree in Project Management. Phillitia is fervently passionate about infusing a message of hope in the lives of youth and women.

Phillitia is a nationally acclaimed educator, author, consultant and life coach. Her mission is to uplift, provoke self-introspection, healing and inspiration. Phillitia has been a school principal for ten years.

CharltonCharlton.com

Phillitia Charlton

Want More of
The Death of a Lie?

Schedule Coffee and Conversation with Phillitia. This powerful message will resonate with youth groups, social organizations, college students, coffee shops, or in your home at your coffee table surrounded by your closest friends.

Coffee and Conversation with Phillitia is a healing circle for readers to delve deeper into the experiences and situations that inspired *The Death of a Lie* poetry collection. Coffee and Conversation with Phillitia encourages readers to identify and acknowledge their own "lies" and ideologies that need to die so the truth can live.

Coffee and Conversation with Phillitia includes an autographed copy of the book, a spoken word reading and facilitation of the book discussion. If you want to extend the conversation, add an affirmation building session. This session will show readers how to create positive affirmation statements to be used as tools to counteract negative thoughts.

To book Phillitia Charlton for a book club discussion, as a keynote speaker, an uplifting motivational speaker or a spoken word artist, log onto <u>CharltonCharlton.com</u> for more information.

The Death of a Lie

For speaking engagements or to order additional copies of

The Death of a Lie

Charlton · Charlton Publishing
PO Box 60671
Dayton, OH 45406
CharltonCharlton.com
937.995.0900

Name

Address

City / State / Zip

(_____)_____

Phone

Email

Quantity	Price Per Book	Total
	$14.95	
Sales Tax (OH residents add $1.08 per book)		
Shipping ($2.99 first book, $0.99 each add'l)		
Grand Total* (Payable to: Phillitia Charlton)		

* Certified check and money orders only
Credit card and Paypal payments accepted online

Available on Amazon.com in paperback and Kindle!

Phillitia Charlton